WA

CELL'*f*
CARE
2

wellness

3 CELL Core Concepts   mo orlovsky   **mo-well.com**

WANT ● WELLNESS

CELL'*f* CARE 2

3 CELL CORE CONCEPTS

because

CELL'*f* Care
is what it all boils down to.

CELL'*f* Care
is 100% dependent on what you:
KNOW right **NOW.**

When you **KNOW**
Your **Body** is made up of **Systems**
Your **Systems** are made up of **Organs**
Your **Organs** are made up of **Tissues**
Your **Tissues** are made up of:
CELLs

**It makes sense that
SELF Care**
is the sum of your

CELL'*f*.

What's mo-well.com all about?
Self (CELL'*f*)Care

Do your CELLs have what they need?

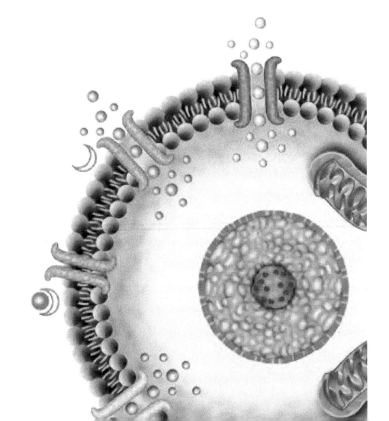

WANT WELLNESS
CELL 'f Care

CELL CORE CONCEPT 1

CELL CORE CONCEPT 2

WANT WELLNESS JOURNEY

CELL CORE CONCEPT 3

INTEGRATED WELLNESS EDUCATORS
i-we.co

WANT WELLNESS BOOKLET SERIES

mo-well.com KNOW blog

CELL'*f*
CARE

CELL

CORE CONCEPT

1

mo orlovsky ● mo-well.com ● i-we.co

CELL CORE CONCEPT 1

Our CELLs are made up of *Systems*.
They are *Integrated*.

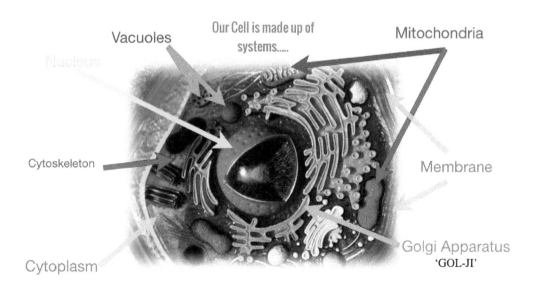

Vacuoles

Our Cell is made up of systems.....

Mitochondria

Nucleus

Cytoskeleton

Membrane

Cytoplasm

Golgi Apparatus
'GOL-JI'

Our Cells are made up of *Systems*.
They are *Integrated*.

Sound familiar?
Yes! **<u>Core Concept 1</u>**: Our **body** is made up of *systems* and they are *integrated*.

How cool is that! Our human organism; made up of all the cells that make our tissues, together making our organs that create our systems... those *very* CELLS have a CELL Core Concept we can already fully understand and appreciate!

The Cell. It is made up of *Systems*.
These *Systems* are called **Organelles**.
(*literally miniature systems*).

CORE CONCEPT 1

Our body is made up of *Systems*.
They are *Integrated.*

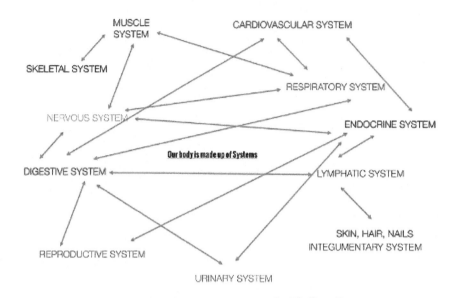

CELL CORE CONCEPT 1

Our CELLS are made up of *Systems*.
They are *Integrated.*

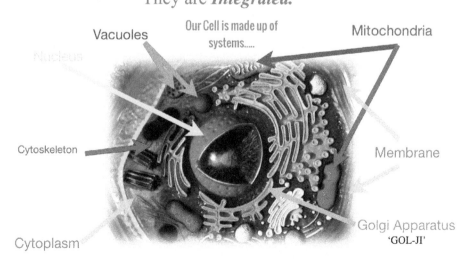

A few cell system examples:

Nucleus: containing the genetic material. It is the largest of the organelles and is identified as the reproductive organelle (system). From here forward I will refer to the cell *organelle* as *system* ;-)

The mitochondria: produces the Cells energy.

The golgi complex gathers simple molecules and combines them making new big molecules, packages them in vesicles, where they either store for later use or sends them out into the cell.

The cytoplasm: jelly like substance giving the cell shape and a space for the organelles to survive and execute their jobs in.

The cytoskeleton the scaffolding that connects all parts of the cell. The cytoskeleton keeps the cell from collapsing: it has many functions just like our bodies skeletal scaffolding like it participates in transporting molecules, coordinates information, regulates genetic expression.

The membrane: is the system of the cell which gives boundary; protection just like our integumentary system *and* it acts as a nervous system evaluating and decision making dependent on it's extracellular environment.

There is so much more but you get the gist.

It's the most amazing thing... each cell system possesses functional equivalents of our Body Systems: our nervous system, digestive system, respiratory system, excretory system, endocrine system, muscle and skeletal systems, circulatory system, integumentary system, reproductive system and even primitive immune system... and it gets better!....

How is that possible!? (*I know you are asking*) How can it be that it gets even better? Well this is going to astound you.

Your cells-- they *are intelligent*!

Just like you and me. They are not just passive things bumping around with no agenda. They are working hard, evaluating, functioning the best they can with survival as their focus.

We are going to delve into that later in the series but for right now lets revel in the fact that since we KNOW it is up to us as KING; from the **WANT WELLNESS**: Cell'*f* Care- 3 Core Concepts; to figure out the **Essentials** to **P**rovide our cells with: it is really helpful for us to KNOW that

    1. our cells have systems that function just like our body's systems.

  2. those cell systems are integrated.

This means although our CELLS are magical and amazing, they are not some mystical thing that is too confusing to figure out how to care for.

On the contrary. We can understand and relate to the CELL Core Concept 1 already because it is the same as our Body Organism Core Concept 1:

' Our Body Organism is made of *Systems*. The Systems are *Integrated*.'

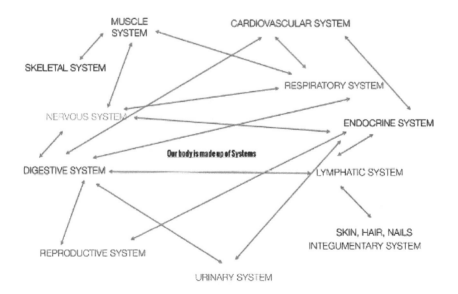

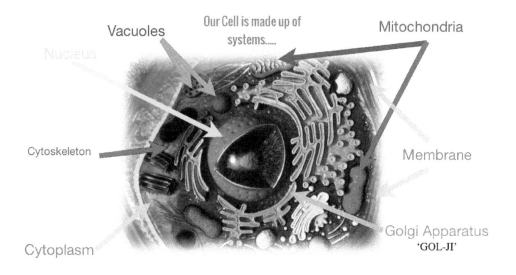

Vacuoles

Our Cell is made up of systems.....

Mitochondria

Nucleus

Cytoskeleton

Membrane

Cytoplasm

Golgi Apparatus
'GOL-JI'

CELL CORE CONCEPT 1

Our CELLs are made
up of *Systems*.
They are *Integrated*.

Our body systems working together create our body.

The same is true for the individual CELLS. Their systems working together create them.

Each Cell is an individual entity. The systems that make up the CELL *are* integrated, *are* interconnected, interdependent, on each other just like our body systems.

To take care of our CELLs we need to KNOW what these systems need.

Looking back at the acronym from WANT WELLNESS: CELL'*f* Care: 3 Core Concepts we know each CELL needs the right **M.E.N.** in their lives to

S.M.I.L.E.: **S**tructure, **M**achinery, **I**nstruction and *lotsa* **E**nergy.

Our focus in WANT WELLNESS: CELL'ƒ Care 2 is to Get to KNOW the 3 **CELL** Core Concepts that will help us with decisions when it comes to **P**roviding the ESSENTIALS the CELLs need. It gives us our guidelines.

Since the WELLNESS we WANT comes down to CELL'ƒ Care this is a really awesome start!

The WELLNESS we WANT is a reflection of the ratio of healthy cells to those that are not.

To take care of ourself we need to KNOW what to **P**rovide our CELLs. In WANT WELLNESS: CELL'ƒ Care - 3 Core Concepts we learned: Core Concept 2: Our Body has a Hierarchy and Our CELLs Rule. That concept places our focus to care for ourself directly on: **P**roviding for our CELLS.

Figuring out how to ***care for our cells*** is easier when we are able to make sense of them! Our first **CELL** Core Concept helps us do that.

CELL CORE CONCEPT 1

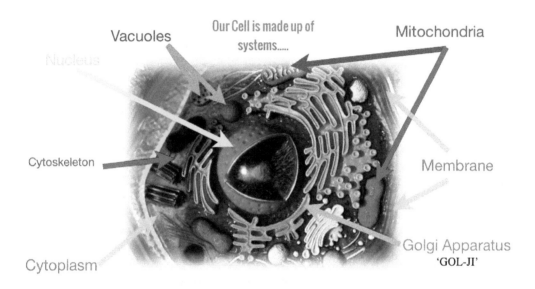

Vacuoles

Our Cell is made up of systems.....

Mitochondria

Nucleus

Cytoskeleton

Membrane

Cytoplasm

Golgi Apparatus
'GOL-JI'

Our CELLs are made
up of *Systems*.
They are
Integrated.

Next up: CELL Core Concept 2:
Where we discover the -

Cellular Organism
has a Hierarchy.

Who do you think
Rules?!

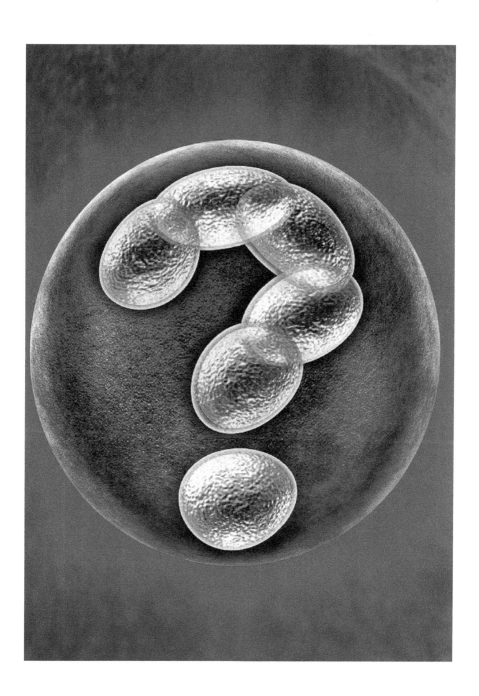

CELL '*f*
CARE

CELL

CORE CONCEPT

2

CELL CORE CONCEPT 2

Our CELLs have a
Hierarchy.
CELL Membranes **Rule**!

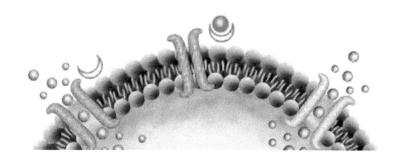

Human Organism Hierarchy

Our human organism is dependent on the health of our CELLS

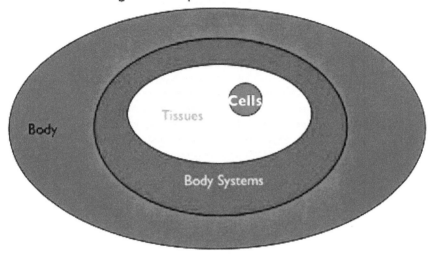

Woohooo! The cell has a hierarchy! Just like us;-) . When it comes to the Human Organism Hierarchy (shown above) it is the CELL that Rules! *Without* the CELLs the Human Organism cannot exist.

When it comes to our CELL Organism; the tiny individual entities they are; with their own integrated systems; *each* is dependent on something too. The CELL Organism like our Human Body Organism; has one thing it is

The Cellular Organism has a Hierarchy

Our Cellular organism is 100% dependent on the health of our membrane

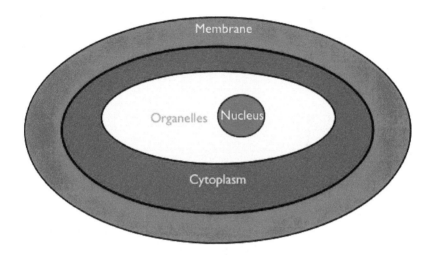

100% dependent on. In the case of our CELLS it is the health of; the integrity of their **CELL MEMBRANE.**

The membrane rules in the CELL Organism hierarchy because without the MEMBRANE the **CELL Organism** *cannot* exist.

The CELL Organism is made up of integrated systems that are dependent on the membrane of the cell. Therefore the CELL Membrane Rules!

Looking at the pictures of the 2 hierarchies it can be confusing as to who rules because of the placement. Many say to me *I thought the Nucleus was what ruled the cell...* I know, I too was taught the Nucleus; housing the genes that 'ran' my cells; was the most important system of the CELL. It is one of the reasons it resonated with me that I just got crappy genes and therefore would go through life 'managing' my body's failures. It was also easy for me to accept this idea of the Nucleus being my WELLNESS Ruler because it was positioned similarly to the CELL in the Human Organism Hierarchy. In my head those two mis-informed ideas created a passive way for me to go about 'managing' my wellness. ***I am so grateful*** to understand CELL Core Concept 2: CELLS have a Hierarchy: Membranes Rule! It changed everything in my thought process.

When it comes to understanding and

Human Organism Hierarchy

Our human organism is dependent on the health of our CELLS

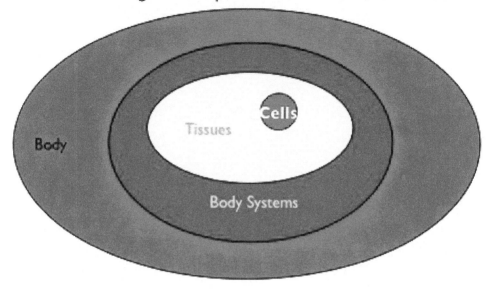

The Cellular Organism has a Hierarchy

Our Cellular organism is 100% dependent on the health of our membrane

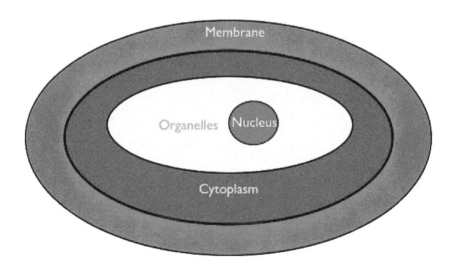

choosing the focus of cellular health ***who rules*** is chosen by identifying what the ORGANISM is 100% dependent on.

For Core Concept 2 and CELL Core Concept 2 the **Ruler** is the *one* thing that determines whether the organism exists or not. *Without* the Ruler the organism would **not exist!**

The Human Body Organism is dependent on the cell which is deepest of the layers of the human organism. We have our Body the outermost layer, then the Systems, then Organs, Tissues, finally CELLS.

Core Concept 2
The Body Organism has a hierarchy:
CELLS Rule!

The CELL Organism, on the other hand, is dependent on the Membrane which is the outermost layer of the CELL Organism.

CELL Core Concept 2
The CELL Organism has a hierarchy:
The Membrane Rules!

Each cell is it's own organism with integrated systems. The Cell Membrane is a cell system with many *many* jobs. As I mentioned; one *very* important job it has is intelligence. The CELL Membrane is the CELL brain!

The Cell uses its membrane to sift through thousands, and thousands of stimuli from their micro environment to select the response with the goal of surviving.

The CELL Membranes are capable of responding to the environment AND are learning through these environmental experiences making memories.

Cellular memories can be passed on for their next generation of cells. This gives *you* a lot of influence, a lot of possibility when it comes to your CELL'*f* Care.

The environmental influence you can have comes down to **P**roviding the **ESSENTIALS-** *those wonderful* **M.E.N.** - influencing your cells!

The ruler title belongs to the CELL Membrane now- but it was not always that way.

Here is what researchers did: They plucked the nucleus out and the cell survived. **It did not reproduce** but it survived. The CELL's Nucleus System, just like *our* Reproductive System, can be removed and still survive.

On the other hand when there was-removal; even severe damage to the Cell Membrane; the Cell did *not* survive.

Membrane rules.

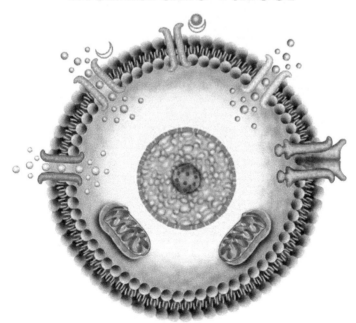

It is the key to cellular wellness.

Remember the CELL Core Concept 2 identifies the organism ruler and the ruler is chosen according to the *hierarchy of existence.*

Our Human Organism is dependent on the CELL.

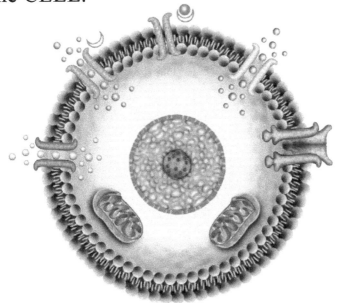

This dependence on the cell places our focus on how to best care for it. KNOWing the **Cell Membrane determines the existence of the Cell**

helps us to pinpoint where to begin our CELL'*f* Care. CELL Core Concept 2 identifies that for us. We begin with the **Cell Membrane**.

The systems that cells have behave and contribute to each cell in similar ways that our body systems behave and contribute to our body.

The Cell systems are interconnected and interdependent on one another which means it behooves us to get to **KNOW** what we can do to make them **S.M.I.L.E.**

It stands to reason the first of the systems to look into whether or not they have what they need to S.M.I.L.E. would be the CELL System that the CELL Organism is 100% dependent on. The CELL Membrane.

Are you Providing your CELL Membranes with what they need?

It is all so logical and yet eludes us as a society because it is simply not brought to our attention to take care of *our* CELL*ves* let alone our CELL Membranes! As a matter of fact many of the 'health' guidelines do exactly the opposite ;-(

How great would that be if we were taught by our pediatricians, when we are old enough to understand we have a body, that we get to help take care of *our*cell*ves*. Nothing more than an introduction which

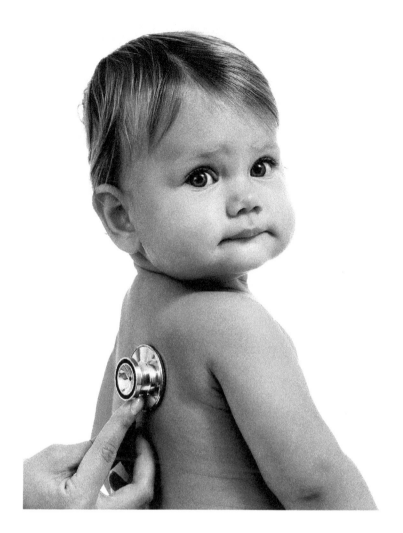

may pique interest, questions of how.

What if we were taught about our CELL
Membrane- just 1 organelle of our CELL

and given the tools, the idea that we can take care of it?

What if we were taught to ask questions like: Does this **M**otion help my CELL Membrane?

Have I taken time; made efforts to reduce the negative physiological response my cells membranes may have to negative **E**motions? If not how can I do that?!

Did I Provide my CELLs Membrane with what they need **N**utritionally today? Have I maybe stressed my CELLs Membrane with consumption of things it does not recognize? need? or with things that it must expend extra energy to recover from?

What specific ESSENTIALS should I try

to incorporate daily for my CELL Membranes?

What if all through our schooling we add a bit more and a bit more (self) CELL'*f* Care information. This repetitive; bite sized pieces of information and exposure would provide us with so much value throughout our lives. Adding an effective tool here and then there.

How wonderful it would be if we were to learn the influence we have on '*our*CELL*f*' by KNOWing a thing or two about what our CELL Membrane needs.

Or professionally; consider the impact our training could have on how we help those who WANT WELLNESS when we go into *any* field of wellness if *basic* CELL'*f* Care was taught.

Minimally KNOWing the CELL Membrane ESSENTIALS and having a health care professional help us incorporate them.

If we all knew from early on what it takes to care for our CELL*ves* and the benefits we could reap I imagine there would be less chronic illnesses.

I KNOW I would have gone about caring for my CELL'*f* differently. Maybe others wouldn't but having the ability; the KNOWing I even had a choice that is where the real empowerment is.

We can only act on what we **KNOW**. Once I knew: Core Concept 3: Cells Rule *but* it was I that was the KING! It was clear that since I was the one **P**roviding for my CELLS I needed to began to **RE**-learn about them.

As I did, it became clearer to me that what *my* cells needed was *no where near being fulfilled by me.*

When I understood that the CELL I was beginning to **P**rovide for -- itself was made up of Systems and that the Systems were integrated: CELL Core Concept 1 and that the CELL Organism was 100% dependent on its CELL Membrane: CELL Core Concept 2

It was this new KNOWing of :

CELL Core Concepts

that helped me BEGIN to change my world from one where I was running after the WELLNESS I WANTED racked with daily suffering....

to one where I was on top of the world....;-)

it helped me think through how to adjust the **M.E.N.** I was **P**roviding my cells.

What we KNOW about our CELL'*f is the key*.

That is exactly the reason the wellness professionals *i-we*.co Foundation Level 1 Course is focused on the **CELL** and the details, mechanisms, ESSENTIALS of its **Care** and why the focus of mo-well.com; the wellness website for all those who WANT WELLNESS; is on **CELL'*f* Care**.

CELL'*f* Care is the basis of *everything* when it comes to attaining the **WELLNESS** we **WANT**.

Our Body Hierarchy, Our Body Systems, Our dependence on our CELLs.

Our CELLs; Their Systems; Understanding they are integrated. Understanding they too have a hierarchy so we can learn where to focus our CELL'ƒ Care.

KNOWing the 3 Core Concepts and the 3 CELL Core Concepts helps us begin the process of KNOWing how to choose the very **ESSENTIALS** we need to Provide our CELL's.

So often; after working with clients Providing the specific ESSENTIALS that had been missing; there ended up being no need to look at their individual systems.

Why? Because when we provide the ESSENTIALS to one cell we are providing for many.

When we provide for the CELLs systems they positively affect many of the CELLs other systems.

We learned this from:

CELL Core Concept 1: CELLs are made up of *Systems*. They are *Integrated*.

and

CELL Core Concept 2: The CELL Organism has a Hierarchy: CELL Membranes Rule!

CELL Core Concept 2 is why the first step I always took with clients was figuring out the missing **ESSENTIALS** specific to *them* that *every* CELL needs **starting** with the needs of the CELL Membrane whenever possible.

That is the work done together in the *Identify Here Process*.

Once we *Identify Here* we can then add the missing **ESSENTIALS** needed by the CELL Membrane that we identified.

The ESSENTIALS that are chosen <u>first</u> come from the list of materials our CELL membrane needs to **S.M.I.L.E.** COOL isn't it!

How do we make
sure our CELLs have
what they need to
S.M.I.L.E.?

We pay attention to
the ESSENTIAL
M.E.N.
in their lives!

Structure
Machinery
Instruction
Lotsa
Energy

Providing the
ESSENTIALS is the
<u>*first*</u> *step* in our WANT
WELLNESS Journey.
Here is what the journey looks like.

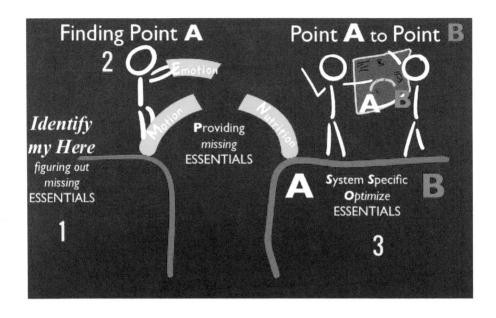

The process of **identifying** the *missing*
Essentials is *Identify HERE (1)*.

Adding the missing ESSENTIALS is called
Finding Point A *(2)*.

It is called **'<u>FINDING</u>' Point A** because with
each ESSENTIAL; that we successfully add;
our body is *finding* its way to our true status:
our **Point A. Point A** is a truer initial wellness
status of our body than one without all the

ESSENTIALS our cells need. Makes sense right. If we are missing key essentials that our cells are dependent on, over time it will negatively impact the tissues, and so on through the hierarchy. When we add an essential we identified as missing and replenish what the cell needs for optimal care and this in return reduces or eliminates a symptom then-- *our body without this symptom* is actually a better picture of our body's true capabilities. The symptom was not because there was

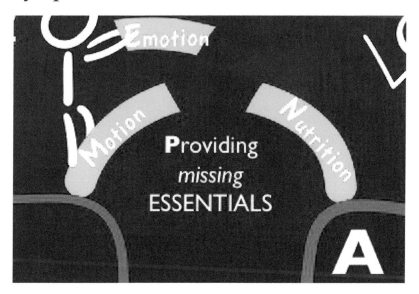

something inherently *wrong* with our body. It was just a 'status' of our body functioning **without** an essential(s). Using me again. There ended up being *nothing wrong* with my Thyroid, my Uterus, my Breasts, my Heart, my Brain,.... all the things I was on medication for *because **'they'** were not working well*. When the essentials were incorporated they all began functioning beautifully! This was my true starting point, my A, from which I could re-evaluate my symptoms and focus on the system(s) that had remaining issues. The idea is we add the next essential and something else melts away **or not**. *This highlights the benefit of adding one essential at a time. And the 60 sec. journaling to refer back to that we use in the ESSENTIALS program.*

Once we add all the missing essentials; arriving at *our* **Point A;** the symptoms that **are hanging on** help us narrow the plan of how we will move forward on our journey. Again, where we _arrive_ **after** adding the ESSENTIALS is **Point A.**

This is where our bio-individuality <u>begins</u> to shine through. Where we will all begin to deviate a bit more when it comes to the personal path toward the WELLNESS we

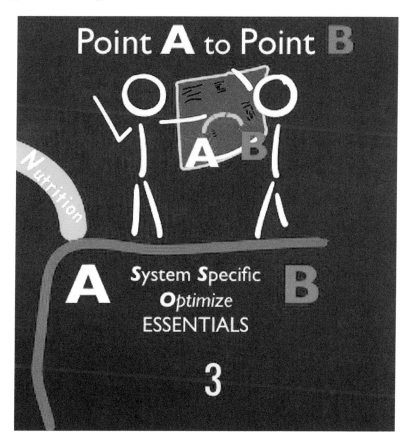

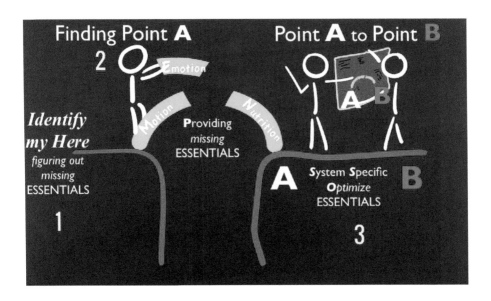

WANT. This brings us to: (*3*) **A** to **B**: **Point A to Point B**: where **System Specifics** is the Focus. There you have it! The **WANT WELLNESS** journey overview.

Identify Here Process and Finding Point A are the concepts in the journey that are least familiar. And as I emphasis in all my *i-we* courses *they are the ones that make the difference for the client*. Skip either and you are just following somebody elses plan.

When we have an issue we typically look to take the action that will make the symptom stop. It is jumping to this place so quickly that can be confusing to our systems.

If we skip taking the time to figure out if the reason a chronic symptom is occurring is due to a lack of an essential or an overburdening of some sort like an environmental toxin causing a greater need of an essential - and instead we seek to stop the signal we are moving further away from our WANT WELLNESS goal and over an extended period of time we begin to place an even greater burden on our CELLs.

I take a lot of time with the journey explanation because making sense of the journey is key to using the Core

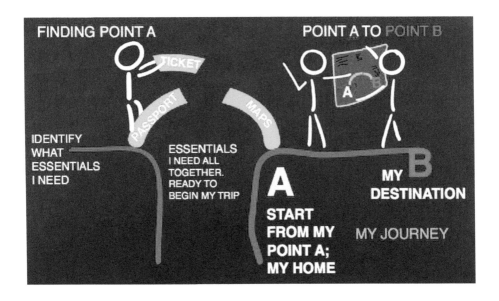

Concepts and CELL Core Concepts.

Often when speaking I swap the words out on the chart and suggest thinking of *Identify Here Process* and **Finding Point A** like this: when we decide to take a journey, we all take similar steps identifying and gathering the essentials needed in order to travel.

We certainly wouldn't skip the steps of figuring out the flight we want to take and purchasing a ticket before going to the airport to leave. It is clear *without the essential items we cannot get very far.*

So we take specific steps:

~ we start by figuring out where we want to go. **(B)**

~ we identify what we have and make a list of what we don't. (:The Core Concept Workbook or our *Identify Here* Process where we are '*Gathering*' pertinent information with an _i-we_.co educator)

~ We begin to get the essentials we identified as missing. (Finding Point A)

~ we consider *where* **we** *are personally starting from:*where is *our* here?our home? Are there additional essentials from this location we need to have **(A)**.

~ once we know the above we begin re-evaluating everything we may need with our new knowledge from our research; are there more *essentials that came to light?* Asking more detailed pertinent questions we have come up with along the way. Is the hotel close by? Far away? Will it take multiple modes of transportation? Tickets? Passport? Visa? A different form of currency? Maps? Actual Guide?

The amount of time; preparation and organization we take to:

*figure out what we are *missing*

*set up the plan to get each of the essentials needed is dependent on the **number** of essentials that are *missing* from the list. Right?.....

If I have a passport I do not need the added 6 weeks of attaining one. I already have the essential. If I have maps from someone who has gone to the destination and can help me with awareness of things to know-

well; their experience and guidance cuts down my research time and so on.

What we all KNOW is we shouldn't leave from our home (Our **Point A**) without our essentials or we will have to circle back to get what we did not take and begin our trip again-. Which of course

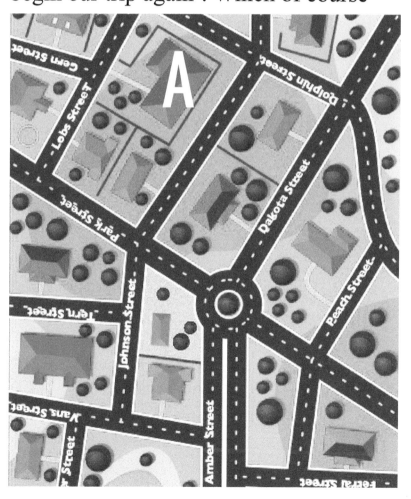

delays our trip if not derails it completely.

If we instead methodically make a plan and assemble the ESSENTIALS we identified as *missing*- it translates into having what *we* need to ultimately have a smoother much more successful trip.

The methodical adding of Cell ESSENTIALS reduces the starting and stopping scenario where we jump over here with excitement to change everything *right now* for the 30 day plan to only find out we stop that too- even if we make the 30 days it doesn't stick. Why? because we did not focus on building the individual CELL'*f* Care essentials that make for a happier you. One that has S.M.I.L.E.s right down to

the core! When we are following *someone elses plan* we have random success- if *our* list of missing *essentials* is different- which is the most likely scenario- we are setting *our*CELL*ves* up to fail by starting off our trip without what <u>we</u> actually need to get to where we are going.

I always encourage clients who seem to

start and stop and start and stop - *a lot* to try and slow things down. I know each and every person will be much closer to the WELLNESS they WANT by adding 1 tiny ESSENTIAL using/doing it daily for 2 weeks *before* adding the next.

It seems slow at first but you build momentum, successes to build on, verses disappointment of *crashing* or *falling off a diet plan* or *exercise regime* you know the typical **here I go**!; **starting today**! *scenarios we all are familiar with.*
The good ole' whack a mole.

There is much more success when you have focused implementation of adding each of the essential M.E.N. you are missing.
With each implementation you are

moving *toward improved* CELL'ƒ Care. The implementation of one ESSENTIAL after another means *1 year from today* your CELLs are getting **22+ *more*** ESSENTIALS than ever before. That is *huuuuge* when it comes to CELL'ƒ Care!

"A year from now you'll wish you started today."

Karen Lamb

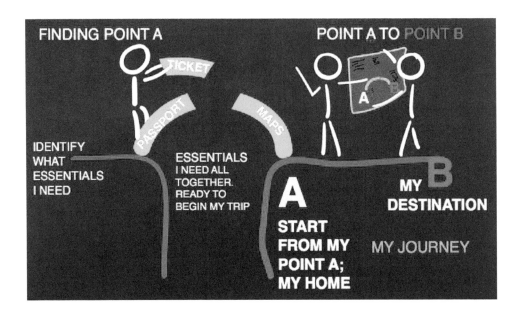

In our trip example- we would not consider going without researching, arranging, packing the essentials we will need, etc. It is also clear; when in this process; that is not until we have *gathered* the information we need, *gathered* all the ESSENTIALS: like our tickets, itinerary, car, place to stay, supplies that we consider ourselves *ready* for the beginning of our trip.

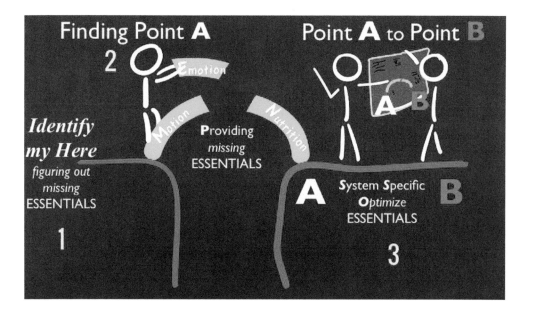

When it is our WANT WELLNESS journey- it is also when ESSENTIALS are all there that we are ready to leave from *our Here* and begin from **Point A**. Remember we want to begin from our Point A because that is a clearer picture of our bodies true capabilities. *That is so important.*

From Point A we to start moving toward our

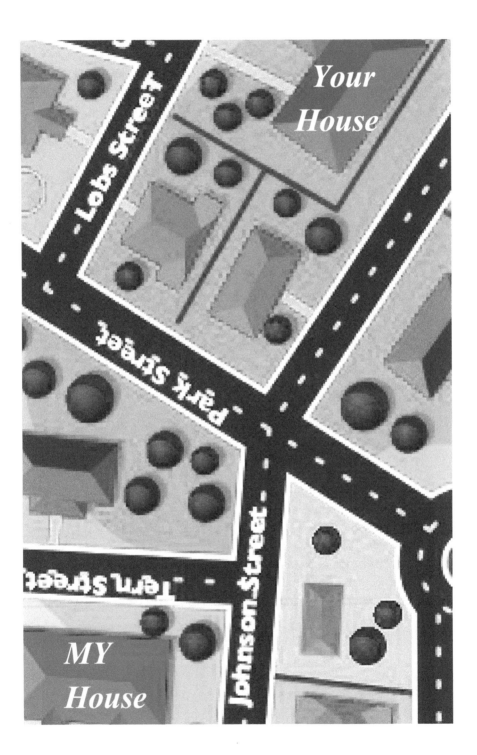

Point B. Adding up experiences and discoveries of our body at its best along the way.

I leave from my house to begin the trip, you leave from yours. We both have the ESSENTIALS we need for the trip, itinerary, tickets, place to stay and so on.

It is the same with the WANT WELLNESS journey. We all need the similar ESSENTIALS to **P**rovide our CELLs with in order to have the best shot at a successful journey.

Once we have **P**rovided our cells with the ESSENTIALS- we begin our bio-individual journey *with* them.

We travel *with* our ESSENTIALS from

our *individual* **Point A to Point B.**

When it comes to our own **WANT WELLNESS** journey it is *while* we are on the journey *from* **Point A** - traveling to our **Point B** that we can begin to understand what *individual* issues *our* body has still sticking around *__after__* we **P**rovided the CELLULAR ESSENTIALS.

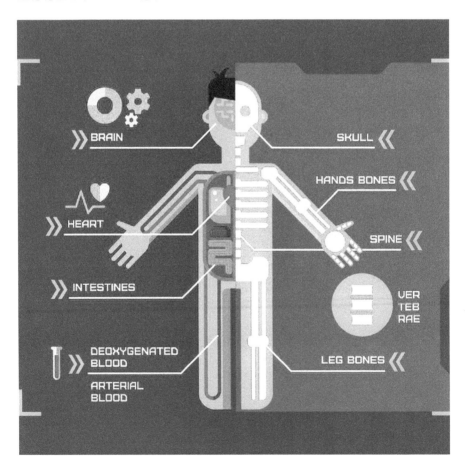

The ESSENTIAL amounts, and specifics that make each of us unique - that is our **Point A to Point B** personal journey.

Staying with the trip theme. You packed all the essentials you planned on needing but it is while you are on your trip **Point A - Point B** that you learn a thing or two about other essentials that make your journey all the better.

You learn things about yourself on the journey that you loved and will be sure to repeat and other things you would not do again.

As the trip goes on you learn that in retrospect you personally needed more of one essential and way less of another essential you packed. You get the idea.

After you gain experience and **P**rovide all

the **ESSENTIALS** over a period of time; your body begins moving toward balancing.

The healthier cells make up more and more of the tissues. Systems begin to respond positively to having healthy cells that make up the very tissues that create the organs that make the specific system.

When every ESSENTIAL is being **P**rovided *yet* a system(s) of the body is not optimizing we look into possibilities of which **M.E.N**. or combination of **M.E.N**. could **P**rovide more of a specific ESSENTIAL to support the specific system(s).
How does our body react when it has maybe *a bit less* of an ESSENTIAL? *a bit more?..*

We refer back to our original collection of body information (*Identify Here*) during this phase *plus* a **Point A to Point B System Specific Intake** if working with *i-we*.co educator.

That sums up the work *from* our **Point A to Point B ;-) Point A to Point B** is where we get System Specific by working with our body signals.

This is how we navigate our **Bio-individual** journey toward the WELLNESS we WANT.

It was only *after* **Providing** my body (remember the **P.O.P.** from WANT WELLNESS: CELL*f* Care: 3 Core Concepts. **Provide** then **Optimize** then **Protect**) that it became clearer what systems of mine could maybe use some added support. Point A to Point B is where I began to **O**ptimize what I **P**rovided for my CELLs.

Looking into the system that needed extra support lead to the uncovering of a genetic system deficiency. Once this deficiency was addressed *waaalaaa*!

Optimization of the **ESSENTIALS** for the problematic system helped to compensate for a deficiency. This Optimization supported multiple systems.. This increased the ability of multiple systems to function at an even more optimal level. For the first time, my body had the opportunity to *begin* to heal and ultimately become healthy.

Over time this lead to my genetically pre-disposed system working optimally-- something it had never done my entire life.

During the healing time it needed more of specific ESSENTIALS for support.
This changed *again* once healed and not further stressed.

As the genetically deficient system got healthier and healthier and it was able to support my other systems as intended.
Then they began to optimize even further!
This again can be attributed to my understanding of:

Core Concept 1 - CELL Core Concept 1 - Core Concept 2 - CELL Core Concept 2

Core Concept 1
My Body is made of Systems
They are *integrated*.

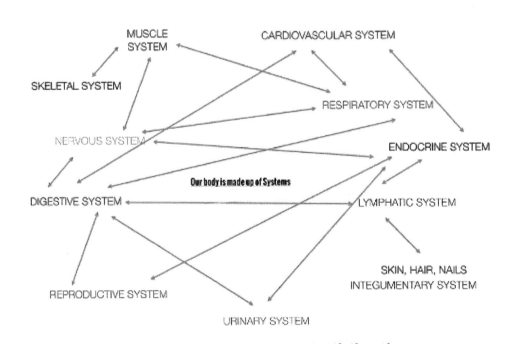

CELL Core Concept 1
My CELL is made up
of Systems
They are *integrated*.

WANT WELLNESS Journey

WANT WELLNESS is a journey not A PATH. Repeatedly **O**ptimizing is part of that journey.

Over time; things change a bit more rapidly because the **O**ptimization of weaker systems start to add up.

For me changes and tweaks were made along the way and by steadily staying engaged with my body; using the 3 Core Concepts and 3 CELL Core Concepts as a framework to guide my next and next decision; my body responded.

Over time the remaining issues of other

systems of mine; that happened to be involved due to the integrated nature of the Human Body Organism; resolved.
It is like they slowly melted away. That is

the best description I can give it. At the start it seemed so very *slooooow* but as I kept to the Core Concepts, CELL Core Concepts as my guideline and focus-**P**roviding the ESSENTIALS I was missing day in and day out the WELLNESS I WANTED began to unfold. The same held true for clients.

The framework; the ability to refer to the Core Concepts and the 3 Core Concepts really made a difference to my Start and Stops: I talked about in WANT WELLNESS: CELL'ƒ Care 3 Core Concepts. When I threw out "MY TIME LINE" that I expected my body to be fixed by I was able to recognize the greater progress that was adding up due to the consistent incorporation of CELL Essentials starting with those the CELL Membrane needed.

This focus; new understanding I had,

eliminated the overwhelm and it all came together. It became easier to figure out the changes and tweaks: the **Point A to Point B** work because I was getting to KNOW my body..

Optimizing the **ESSENTIALS** I **P**rovided using both: CELL Core Concept 1 and CELL Core Concept 2 KNOWledge to help guide my decisions. I arrived at my **Point B!**

MY destination!

Core Concept 2

The Body Organism has a *Hierarchy*

CELLs *RULE!*

and

CELL Core Concept 2

Our CELLs have a *Hierarchy.*

CELL Membranes **Rule**!

KNOWing CELL Core Concept 2 was the very first time I made a wellness decision around my CELL. Specifically around my **CELL Membrane**.

It was when I understood *my* Self Care was a **SUM** of *my* CELL'*f* Care that I began; with razor sharp focus; **P**roviding the support of daily incorporation of ESSENTIALS I *Identified* my CELL Membrane was missing. This one focused decision around the health of my CELL's Ruler- it's Membrane helped me to make better and better decisions when it came to my CELL'*f* Care.

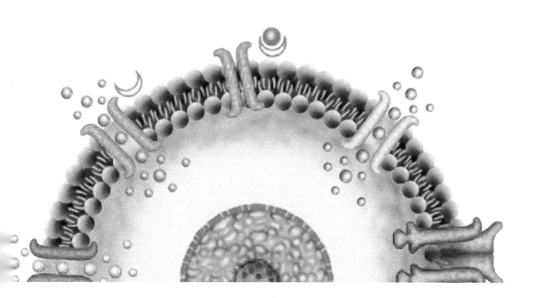

CELL'*f*
CARE

CELL

CORE CONCEPT

3

~ The **King** of the
3 Cell Core Concepts ~
Wanna guess who is KING?

CELL CORE CONCEPT 3

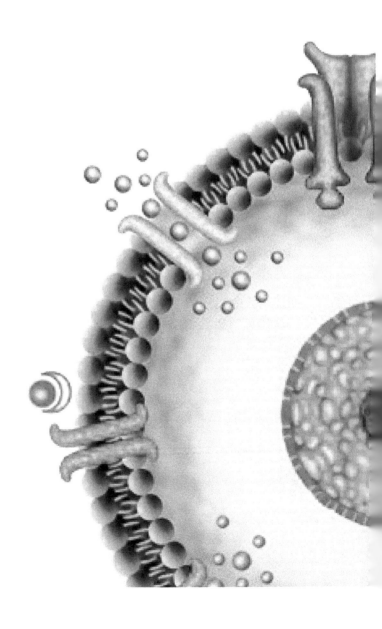

CELL Membranes **Rule**
but
<u>YOU</u> are *KING*!

Cell*f* Core Concept 3: CELL Membranes Rule but <u>YOU</u> are **KING!** The King of the 3 Cell Core Concepts revealed.

CELL Core Concept 1: Cells have systems; they are integrated.

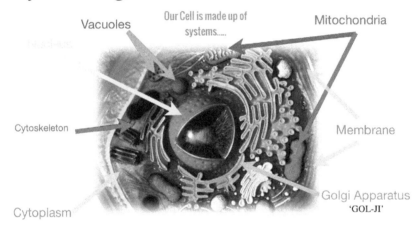

CELL Core Concept 2: Cells Organism has a hierarchy: Cell membranes rule!

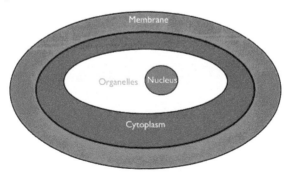

The Membrane rules.

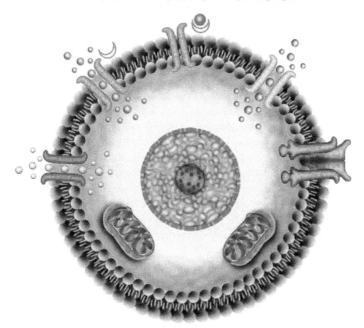

It is the key to cellular wellness.

Cell membrane integrity and health is key to *our cells health.*

Just like our Human Body Organism the Cell Membranes are affected by their environment. Their environment is modulated by **M**otion, **E**motion, and **N**utrition. This brings us to identifying who is in control of the **M.E.N.** Who is KING when it comes to the CELL

Membrane?

Cell membranes rule but ultimately it is
YOU that still remains KING.

'**YOU**; are the ruler. **You** are King.
You have the GREATEST influence on the
environment of your cell membranes.

We have our **body**
Made up of **integrated systems**
Those systems are made up of **organs**
The organs are made up of **tissues**
Our tissues made up of **cells**
Cells rule. **Period.**

Our **cells** are made up of **systems**
Those systems are **integrated.**
The **Cell Membrane** is a CELL System.
Our *cells* existence *depends* upon its **Cell
membrane**.
Cell membranes rule. **Period.**

But

it is '**YOU**; that remains the ***KING!***
YOU have the influence on the ruler of your
cell. How is that? Well, the cell membrane is
dependent on _you!_ *That makes _YOU_* **King**.
Isn't that great! It's not *just* dumb luck or only
your genetics.

You have influence!

CELL Core Concept 3: is the **King** of the 3 CELL Core Concepts: The other 2 CELL Core Concepts are very important to understand but King of CELL Concepts is CELL Core Concept 3 because the CELL Membrane is dependent on *you*.

YOU are **King**. You decide what the cell membrane gets and what you do with the experiences it processes or not.
You decide it's resources, how it is treated, it's life style per se. You control it's environment that it is 100% dependent on.

Your cell and your cells membrane are separate yet inseparable.

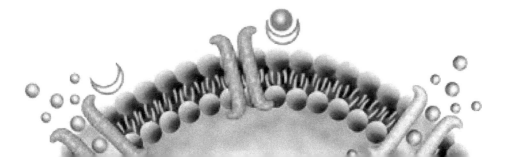

Your cell is 100% dependent on the cell membrane.

~

The cell membrane is 100% dependent on YOU!.

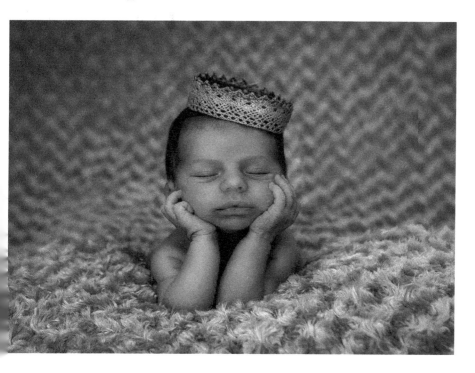

You are the gatekeeper.
*You get to **P**rovide your CELL membrane with what it needs.*

I was so relieved when I figure this out. And it is comforting to me even today.

These guidelines stemming from CELL Core Concept 1, 2 & 3 are with me still. Every single day. They remain key in my decisions and ability to **Protect** the WELLNESS I achieved. **P**rotect being the last of the **P.O.P.**

3 Core Concepts and 3 CELL Core Concepts make it possible to begin to understand and engage in the processes of the WANT WELLNESS journey we mapped out in the last section:

Identifying YOUR Here

Finding **Point A**

Point A to **Point B**

The process of **WANT WELLNESS:** CELL'ƒ Care. *Taken out of order doesn't work.*

If we do not *Identify our Here* then start **Finding Point A** by **P**roviding our Cells with the missing **ESSENTIALS** <u>first</u> but instead pick out one of our systems *that seems* like it needs extra support; which is basically what our model is now- oh this thing in my body is wrong - I'll *try this because "the newest study says"...,NOW this **and that** is wrong!- I guess I will try **this and that** because it is known to help my friend....the whack-a-mole approach.....*

...we may actually be *stressing* multiple of our CELLS systems-- *not* helping them.

I KNOW that is what happened to me year in and year out always chasing after the WELLNESS I WANTED only to have more and more of my systems stressed past their limit.

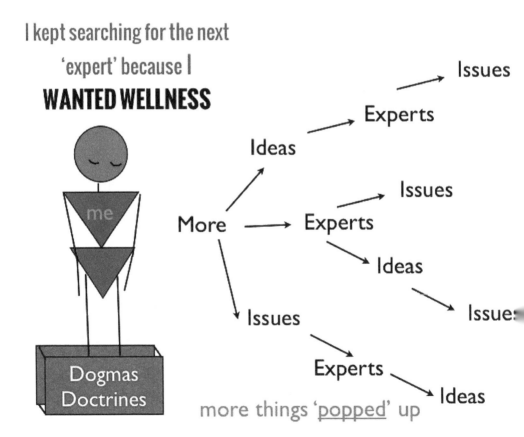

Here is an example where I wish I knew the 3 Core Concepts and 3 CELL Core Concepts-

I took a particular dietary approach that was suggested to me and incorporated it because of course I WANTED WELLNESS and the Nutritionist at the hospital had very specific suggestions. The suggestions were also in line with the college nutrition education I received. *Couldn't hurt right.*

BOY was I wrong! Remember at this point I did not KNOW the 3 Core Concepts or the 3 CELL Core Concepts **and** we can only make decisions on what we KNOW right!?!

Here is where KNOWing Core Concept 1, 2 , 3 *and* CELL Core Concept 1, 2 & 3 would have kept me from harming *my*CELL'*f* and delaying getting the WELLNESS I WANTED.

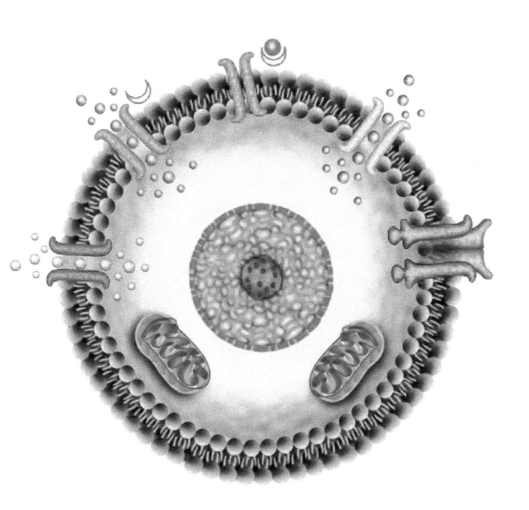

By diligently changing my diet, unbeknownst to me, I eliminated not 1 but 2 CELL ESSENTIALs.

Had I; the KING of my CELLS; understood they were ESSENTIALs for *multiple systems* in the CELL I would have recognized it as a bad idea.

Had I; King of the CELL Membrane: understood they were ESSENTIALs for the RULER of the CELL - the CELL Membrane - I would have _never_ entertained the idea.

But because I did not have the Core Concept and CELL Core Concept filters that *one* dietary change of 2 ESSENTIALS *reduced* the health of my CELLS even further from where I started from. (*which was a pretty sorry place to begin with*).

It was that whack a mole process. I was just going to 'try' it because I was told it would help. Lotsa studies to back it up *and* I WANTED WELLNESS!

I know you know what happened- the missing ESSENTIALs - KEY in the health of my **CELLs Membranes**; *those ESSENTIALS I was diligently avoiding because I was told 'studies show' it would be good for my health;*

well in retrospect it is clear what I was doing was the key to an even more rapid deterioration of my health. Moving me even further away from the WELLNESS I WANTED.

It's negative impact on my CELL Membranes resulted in a negative impact on *multiple* systems of my cells since the Membrane Rules and the CELLs are integrated. I needed more specialists, more prescriptions to manage my young body.

Here I was getting more and more upset at my body for 'failing' me when I was in complete control of taking out the ESSENTIALs crucial to my CELL Membranes well being.

The moment I understood **CELL Core**

Concept 2: The Cell Organism has a hierarchy and Membranes Rule! A light bulb went off:

'*Was I* **Providing** *my* **CELL Membranes** *with the* **ESSENTIAL M.E.N.** *needed.!?*'

A big FAT <u>NO</u>!

I was devastated. Not only was I *missing* some ESSENTIALS I was ***purposely* avoiding** the very **ESSENTIALS my CELL Membrane** needed most! The sad thing is a *majority* of us are doing that! Avoiding CELL Membrane ESSENTIALS thinking we are caring for ourselves ;-(

<u>UGH</u>!!!

Those days are gone! K nowing **NOW:**
(name of blog at mo-well.com) K NOW

The 3 Core Concepts:

1. The Body is made of Systems; the Systems are integrated.

2 The Human Body Organism has a Hierarchy: CELLs Rule!

3. CELLs Rule BUT You are KING!

The 3 CELL Core Concepts:

1. The CELL is made of Systems: They are integrated.

2. The CELL Organism has a Hierarchy; CELL Membrane Rules!

3. Our CELL Membrane rules! BUT it is YOU that are KING!

means *every study*, *piece of advice*, *the next 'thing'* **ALL** of it -I can *think it through*. Does the advice help me Care for my CELL'*f*?
The Core Concept and CELL Core Concept CELL'*f* Care knowledge is always helping me make the best decisions I can.

...avoiding the negative impact the whack a mole approach had to offer me.

The Membrane rules.

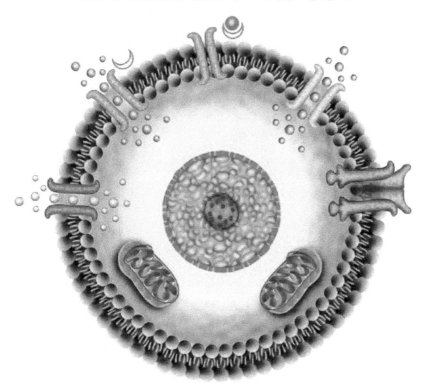

It is the key to cellular wellness.

I have learned to aim to discover and **Provide ESSENTIALS** first to the CELLs Membranes.

This one focus turns out time and time again to have a positive effect on all the CELL Systems. When the Membranes have all the raw materials **Provided**: the right **M.E.N.** in their lives: they can better **Provide**, **Protect** and **O**ptimize the other Systems of the CELL.

When we apply: CELL Core Concept 1: Our Cells are made up of Systems; they are *integrated* and CELL Core Concept 2: Our Cells have a Hierarchy; *Cell Membrane* Rules!: to how *we as* **King:**

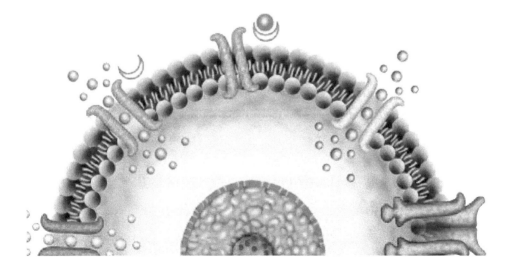

CELL Core Concept 3 care for *ourCELLves it is logical* we will do the most good <u>across the entire body</u>.

As King **P**roviding the missing **ESSENTIALS** to our Cells Membrane is our first line of duty.

Focus on Individual Systems: *after* CELLs **ESSENTIALS** our second.

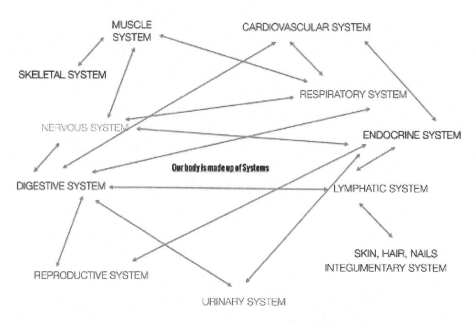

every system is *integrated* with the others

i-wee

Re-cap:

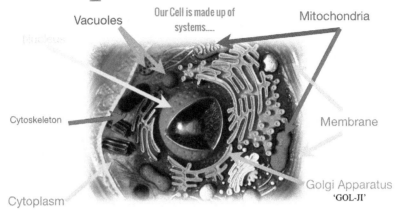

Vacuoles

Our Cell is made up of systems.....

Mitochondria

Nucleus

Cytoskeleton

Membrane

Cytoplasm

Golgi Apparatus
'GOL-JI'

Our Cells are made up of systems; these systems help the cell to move materials throughout their cellular body, breakdown and use materials to feed themselves, eliminate what they do not need, are affected by hormones, have protective layers and can adapt to their environment, they have memory and, and and....*so cool!*

The fact that **Core Concept 1** is identical to our body's **Cell Core Concept 1** makes it relatable, understandable.

CELL Core Concept 1

The CELL is made of *Systems* they are *Integrated.*

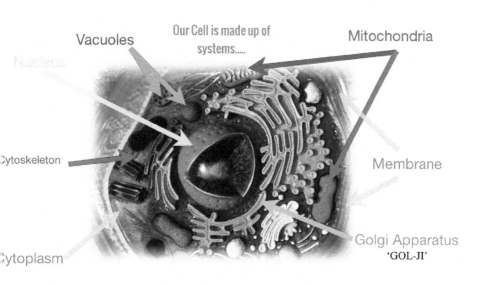

Vacuoles

Our Cell is made up of systems.....

Mitochondria

Nucleus

Cytoskeleton

Membrane

Cytoplasm

Golgi Apparatus
'GOL-JI'

Our **Body** is made up of *Systems*.
The Systems are *Integrated*.

Our **CELL** is made up of *Systems*.
The Systems are *Integrated*.

It was so hard to contain my excitement of this whole realization that our cells are like mini ***us*** - so many times people have come up to me and said

" *mo* the first realization of Core Concept 3 that ***I*** was KING. That I was the one in charge of my CELLs--- *that* was exciting **BUT** I was blown away by understanding **CELL Core Concept 1, 2 and 3**: that the simple act of **P**roviding my CELLs;

especially the CELL Membrane; with ESSENTIALS- would be so powerful across the Cell--*that* was SUPER empowering!

It made the WELLNESS I WANT feel more attainable. It made it feel like I could actually DO THIS.

I feel like *I now* **KNOW** what I **P**rovide for my cells truly has implications and impact. It is not just some foreign idea about taking care of myself any more. Or sticking to a plan. It is about CELL'*f* Care.

After this Seminar I KNOW if I **P**rovide the specific ESSENTIALS my CELLs are currently missing--- it will *positively* affect

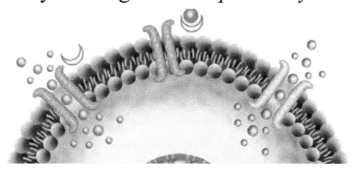

the integrated cellular systems. I am extremely motivated now to understand what ESSENTIALS I **P**rovide and figure out which ones are missing."

It is moments like those where I think to myself: AWESOME!

It is exactly why I do what I do. And why I want to pass on what I do before leaving the field to retire.

To see the light bulbs go off as they did for me and later hear the wonderful transformations people have had. It doesn't get better than that!

NOW you are in the KNOW

Just two **WANT WELLNESS: CELL'*f* Care** kindle booklets into the wellness that you want and a whole new way to look at how to go about getting it.

Now that you KNOW your **Cells** are *also* shaped by the **M.E.N.** in their lives.

You KNOW that the cells *environment* will either help promote them to be fulfilled, healthy, strong and have what they need to **S.M.I.L.E.** (the acronym presented in WANT WELLNESS CELL'ƒ Care) or not.

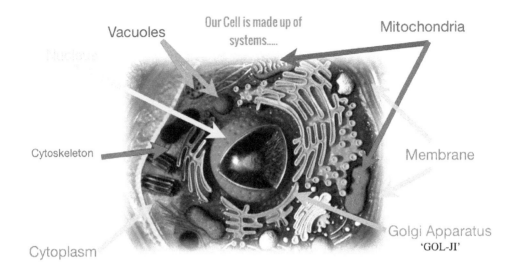

Our Cell is made up of systems.....

Vacuoles

Mitochondria

Nucleus

Cytoskeleton

Membrane

Cytoplasm

Golgi Apparatus
'GOL-JI'

Structure

Machinery

Instruction

***L**otsa*

Energy

This makes it time to move forward to the next step in our WANT WELLNESS journey. To uncover the new understanding of the CELL membrane. It's jobs, what the CELL Membrane is made of so we can begin understanding the ESSENTIAL **M.E.N** to place our focus on. You will find that in **WANT WELLNESS**: CELL'*f* Care: ESSENTIALS 1.

WANT WELLNESS: Cell*f* Care 2 -
3 <u>CELL</u> Core Concepts.

CELL Core Concept 1 Our Cells are made up of systems they are integrated.

CELL Core Concept 2 The Cell has a Hierarchy and the Cell membrane rules.

CELL Core Concept 3 *the King of the 3 Cell Core Concepts*. Cell membranes rule but ultimately it is **YOU** that still remains **KING.**
You are the one in control.

On mo-well.com I have created the

*K*NOW blog- for you as ongoing support.

There will always be **3 CELL ESSENTIAL** Posts.

1 **M.** *motion*

1 **E.** *emotion*

1 **N.** *nutrition*

Plus 1 Feature; in depth post;

on a **CELL'*f* Care topic**.

When a new CELL ESSENTIAL or Feature CELL'*f* Care topic post is added - the older one will be moved out. This is to keep the material very focused.

Regardless of when the first day is that you first visit *KNOW* -by beginning to incorporate 1 CELL ESSENTIAL then adding the next one 2 weeks later- **a year from today** *you* will have incorporated 22+ CELL ESSENTIALS for your **CELL'*f* Care**.

That is 22+ ESSENTIALS you will be *Providing your CELLs* with. Done in a way that was completely doable and therefore now a part of your **CELL'*f* Care**.

That is amazing! **AND** it is by far the best WAY to begin the type of **CELL'*f* Care** it takes to attain the **WELLNESS** you **WANT**. The *KNOW* blog is the ongoing support of the **WANT WELLNESS: CELL'ƒ Care** kindle booklet series. Get on the <u>KNOW</u> list!

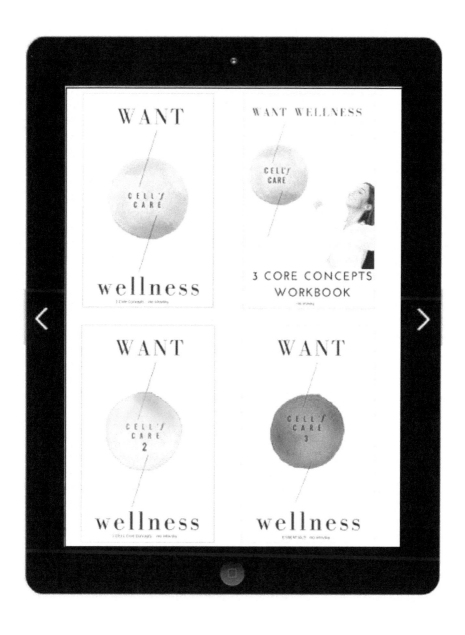

Self Care is the sum of
CELL*'f* Care.

YOU'VE GOT THIS!

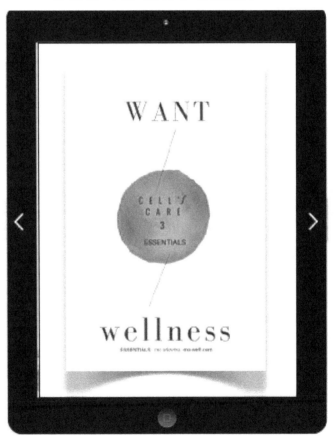

Begin **WANT WELLNESS**: CELL*'f* Care
ESSENTIALS 1. Today!

If you happen to be looking for Identify Here Process and Finding Point A guidance an *i-we: integrative wellness educator* Level 1 is right for you.

Submit your request for possibilities to connect here. - I would like to explore the possibility of connecting- I am happy if I can be helpful in making a connection.

Once the **ESSENTIALS** have been **P**rovided for a while *i-we*.co Foundation Level 2 educators have the tools for Individual System **Point A to Point B** discovery.

Submit your request for possibilities to connect here. - I would like to explore the possibility of connecting with *i-we* Level 2 professional- I am happy if I can be helpful in making a connection.

LINK SUMMARY PAGE

mo-well.com facebook

mo-well.com K**NOW** blog subscribe

i-we.co facebook

i-we.co website

i-we.co Courses

i-we.co educator connect request

Back System info

ESSENTIALS 2 Protein Interest

Interest in Omega 6 Omega 3 ratio

Post Updates: The *Newest* Study Says...

POST:Stop Inflaming yourCELL'f with Healthy Oil

WANT WELLNESS WORKBOOK & TOOLS

To place yourself on a *general* list as new books; webinars or courses are produced use this link. You will be notified the moment new information is available.

 WANT WELLNESS:CELL'*f* CARE

Lightning Source UK Ltd.
Milton Keynes UK
UKHW020925300519

343587UK00009B/190/P